This Little Prayer of Mine

Anthony DeStefano

illustrated by Mark Elliott

HARVEST HOUSE PUBLISHERS
EUGENE, OREGON

This book is for my nephew and namesake,
Anthony Joseph Fagundes.
        —Anthony DeStefano

This book is for William Joseph Elliott,
nephew and teacher—and for all teachers
everywhere, big and small.
        —Mark Elliott

I know you're up in heaven, God,
and can hear my voice from there.

I'm just a little child.

Will you answer my short prayer?

Whenever I feel really scared
and want to hide my head,

please help me to be brave and strong
and face my fears instead.

And when my heart is very sad
and tears roll down my face,

please help me to be happy
so a smile can take their place.

Whenever I feel all mixed up,
unsure of what to do,
please show me what the right path is
and help me follow you.

And when I act a little bad,
not like I know I should,

forgive me, God.
Please don't be mad
and help me to be good.

Whenever I feel all alone
with not a friend in sight,
please let me know you're
here with me
and everything's all right.

Now if I'm being selfish, God,
by asking for too much,
I'd like to tell you thank you
for a bunch of other stuff.

For toys and rides and candy
and Christmas bells that ring.
For summertime and wintertime,
for autumn and the spring.

For puppies, pies, and ice cream,
my family and my friends.

But most of all, I'm grateful
for your love that never ends.

Please help me, God,
to be like you.

Give me your love to share.

I want to help the poor and sick
and show them that I care.

And if you give me riches, God,
that fill a treasure chest,
I promise to be generous
and share what I possess.

I don't know what the future holds

or what's in store for me.

Right now I'm just
a little kid
and don't know what to be.

I might become a movie star.
I might play in a band.

Who knows? I might be president
and rule this great big land.

But when I trust in you, my God,
and in your plan for me,
I know there's nothing in the world
that I can't do or be.

So now this little prayer of mine
is coming to an end.
There's really just one other thing
I'd like to ask again.
Please love me, God, forevermore.
That's all I want.
Amen.

This Little Prayer of Mine

Text copyright © 2010 by Anthony DeStefano
Illustrations copyright © 2010 by Mark Elliott

Published by Harvest House Publishers in 2014
Eugene, Oregon 97408
www.harvesthousepublishers.com

ISBN 978-0-7369-5861-5

Design and production by Katie Brady Design, Eugene, Oregon

Previously published by Waterbrook Press, Colorado Springs, Colorado, in 2010

Printed in China

20 21 22 / LP / 6 5 4 3 2